All About Plants

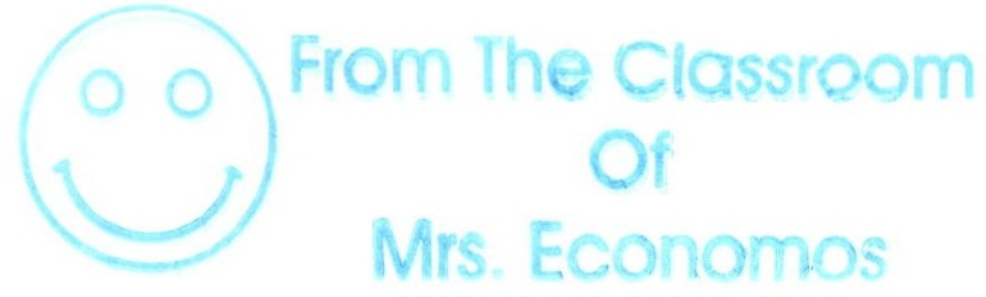

SCHOOL PUBLISHERS

Orlando Austin New York San Diego Toronto London

Visit *The Learning Site!*
www.harcourtschool.com

What Plants Need

Plants make their own food.
They need light and air.

Plants need water and nutrients.
Plants use these things to make food.

Roots

Roots take in water and nutrients. Roots also help hold a plant in soil.

Stems

Stems hold up the plant.
Food and water move through stems.

Leaves

Leaves take in light and air.
Leaves use light and air to make food.

Flowers, Fruits, and Seeds

Flowers make fruits.
Seeds grow in the fruit.

How Plants Grow

Most plants grow from seeds.
A seed coat protects the seed.

Inside the seed is a tiny plant.
It needs warmth and water to grow.

Grouping Plants

Grasses are a group of plants.
Trees are another group.

Edible plants are a group.
Nonedible plants are another group.

Vocabulary